Inspiration-
Love,
Stacey

# The Four Seasons of Love

# THE FOUR SEASONS OF LOVE

### Lorraine Bodger

**Andrews McMeel**
**Publishing**

Kansas City

05 06 07 08 09 WKT 10 9 8 7 6 5 4 3 2 1

ISBN-13: 978-0-7407-5461-6
ISBN-10: 0-7407-5461-0

Library of Congress Control Number: 2005921769

Illustrations by Lorraine Bodger
Book design by Holly Camerlinck

www.andrewsmcmeel.com

# INTRODUCTION

The year turns—golden summer, crisp autumn, cozy winter, tender spring—and each season brings its pleasures and delights for lovers. No season lacks opportunity for love and romance; every season is a time for celebration, a time to enjoy each other and the world you make together.

The seasons are a wonderful metaphor for love—constant, eternal, yet always changing. They bring variety, excitement, and fun to our lives, just as love does. You resist them at some times, embrace them at others. You look forward to one season and feel a little wistful as it gradually transforms itself into the next season—but you also anticipate its certain return. Is love any different?

The very best you can do for yourself in life is to fling yourself wholeheartedly into the unique pleasures of each month of the year and live fully in every magical moment. This is true of love as well. Put the two together and you have *The Four Seasons of Love.*

So fill your lover's calendar with joy (and kisses!), and don't let a day go by without showing your devotion to the one you cherish most. Treasure *every* season. Make plans, make love, make memories.

# SUMMER *Love*

Summer is playful—the fun season of the year. Where does love fit in? Everywhere! The cottage at the lake, the cabin in the woods, Saturdays at the seashore, weekend getaways for just the two of you, long vacations together far from home. Drive-in movies and backyard pools, theme parks and outdoor concerts, frosty summer drinks on the terrace, a hammock under the trees—so many romantic things to do in the golden sunshine and flower-bright colors of summer.

Make your summer a summer of love. Get married in a fragrant green garden under a cobalt blue sky. Take your sweetheart on a perfect picnic or woo him with a cool summer drink at twilight. Wear something bare and sexy, dance under the stars, go skinny-dipping. Croon a love song to your darling or treat her to an old-fashioned romantic movie. Shower your love with June blossoms, July fireworks, and August love tokens. Let the heat of summer add spice to your romance, and enjoy every minute of it.

# Contents

# Remembering Summer Loves

It's the first deep blue, star-lit, meltingly warm, deliciously scented night of true summer. You stand at your window, on your balcony, on the front porch, in the backyard—and suddenly you're thrust back in time. You're overcome with memories of a long-lost summer love you rarely think about now. Someone to whom you gave your whole heart. Someone you couldn't wait to see every day of one magical July or August. Someone who made your pulse race and your skin tingle. You waited for the phone call, the knock on your door, the sound of the voice you longed to hear more than anything else.

Years have passed. You've moved on. You don't even know where your once-beloved now lives. But this enchanted summer night has brought your summer lover back to you on the strong wings of memory. It's melancholy and sweet at the same time, a precious moment to cherish—and then to let go.

## All-Time Great Romantic Movies

When summer puts you in the mood for romance, but you want to stay inside your house where the air-conditioning will keep things cool enough for hot snuggling, pop one of these old-fashioned romantic movies into that new-fangled machine.

| | |
|---|---|
| *The Long Hot Summer* | *Gone with the Wind* |
| *A Summer Place* | *Casablanca* |
| *Splendor in the Grass* | *An Affair to Remember* |
| *Summertime* | *The African Queen* |
| *Roman Holiday* | *The Philadelphia Story* |
| *Breakfast at Tiffany's* | *Some Like It Hot* |

*Sabrina* (the original!)

# From Your Flower Garden

You've made a spectacular summer garden. It's brilliant with color and the fragrance is luscious; bees are buzzing contentedly, butterflies dance and flirt like pretty girls at a party. Zinnias, daisies, marigolds, peonies, petunias, sweet peas, snapdragons, roses, lilies, lobelia, gardenias, gladioli, pansies, alyssum, sunflowers, cornflowers, heather, honeysuckle, hollyhocks, and delphiniums—such lovely names, such lovely flowers.

Take time to enjoy your garden. True, it blooms every year, but a garden is like love—not a moment of it should be wasted. Give attention to your garden—cultivate it, care for it, admire it. Share your garden—bring bouquets to your sweetheart every day, picnic in it à deux, sip wine together while the sun sets and the changing light plays over the blossoms. Your garden is a romance with the senses, and there's nothing sweeter than spending time there with your beloved.

mint

sage

# From Your Herb Garden

Herbs have traditional meanings and mythical powers for lovers. Grow them as plants or pots—grow lots! They add savor and relish to food (and life). Run your hands firmly over the leaves and then sniff your palms—instant fragrance, fresh and delicious. Let your lover sniff, too . . . mmm, maybe a little kiss on that sweet-smelling palm?

thyme

parsley

- ❀ Rosemary, for remembrance
- ❀ Chervil, for sincerity
- ❀ Sage, for wisdom and esteem
- ❀ Summer savory, for mental powers (cast a spell on him!)
- ❀ Mint, for virtue and lust (and for juleps)
- ❀ Lovage (the herb with *love* built right in), for love
- ❀ Thyme, for courage—and love
- ❀ Basil, for devotion—and love
- ❀ Parsley, for festivity—and love!
- ❀ Marjoram, for happiness—and (guess what) love!

rosemary

lovage

# Love at the Beach

Splash in the sea or the lake together. Float on your backs, holding hands so you don't lose each other in the vastness. Dive underwater and kiss, kiss, kiss. Watch the sunset, cuddling as the air cools and the night falls gently. Lie on a blanket in the dark and find the constellations. Skinny-dip. Drink chilled wine and eat delicious tidbits. Stay until morning to welcome the sunrise. Be in the moment—there will never be another day exactly like this one.

# The Greatest Rock 'n' Roll Hits of Summer

Remember these, the all-time greatest hits that captured the very essence of summer? You rocked, you rolled, you danced cheek-to-cheek, crazy about your latest flame. Summer would never end, you'd never have to part. Then July slid past, August was gone, and pretty soon your summer romance faded away, along with those tearful promises of undying devotion and the letters you never did write. But the music lived on, a poignant reminder of the fun you had and the love you lost.

- "Lazy, Hazy, Crazy Days of Summer"
- "Under the Boardwalk"
- "Up on the Roof"
- "Summer in the City"
- "In the Summertime"
- "Love Letters in the Sand"
- "A Summer Song"

# Summer Wedding Bells

Glorious summer is a perfect time for a wedding and reception. The sun shines on you and yours, blessing your union, and you're as blissfully happy as you've ever imagined you could be.

Marry in a garden shaded by old and beautiful trees, surrounded by the heady scent and rainbow colors of flowers. Marry on a white sand beach, in a fresh sea breeze, looking out at the tranquil water and far horizon. Marry in church, with cascades of white blossoms everywhere and jewel-colored light pouring in through the stained-glass windows. Receive your guests under a brightly striped tent and regale them with savory delicacies and icy champagne. Have an old-fashioned barbecue, a picnic in a grassy meadow, a buffet on the roof at dusk. Dance till dawn.
Be joyous and celebrate your love.

# Summer Picnic for Two

Wait for a sunny summer Saturday and get up early (while it's still cool) to prepare this delicious lunch. Grab your sweetie and hightail it out of town for a picnic. Any spot will do—a meadow, à park, a lake, a beach—as long as the two of you are alone together.

## MENU

Chilled Tomato-Basil Soup (page 12)

Deviled Chicken Salad (page 13)
on tender lettuce leaves

Rolls or biscuits

Fruit sorbet in ice cream cones

Sand cookies

Lemonade, wine

# Chilled Tomato-Basil Soup

**1¹/₂ pounds ripe tomatoes**

**Small clove garlic**

**¹/₄ cup chopped onion**

**³/₄ cup chicken broth**

**¹/₂ cup evaporated milk**

**1¹/₂ teaspoons sugar**

**1 tablespoon chopped fresh basil**

**Salt, fresh pepper**

Peel the tomatoes, core, and cut in half across the equator. Gently squeeze out the juice and seeds through a strainer set over a small bowl. Reserve the tomatoes and juice; discard the seeds.

Puree half the tomatoes with the juice, garlic, onion, broth, milk, and sugar. Pour into a large bowl. Chop the remaining tomatoes and add them to the bowl, along with the chopped basil and salt and pepper to taste. Serve chilled.

# Deviled Chicken Salad

**¹/₄ pound baby green beans (haricots verts), stemmed and cut into 1¹/₂-inch lengths**

**2 whole chicken breasts, poached, skinned, boned, and cut into ¹/₂-inch pieces**

**1¹/₂ tablespoons white wine**

**¹/₃ cup sour cream**

**2 tablespoons mayonnaise**

**1 tablespoon Dijon mustard**

**¹/₂ teaspoon powdered dried tarragon**

**Salt, fresh pepper**

Blanch the beans for 1 minute. Drain, rinse in cold water, and pat dry on paper towels. In a large bowl, toss the beans with the chicken.

Make the dressing: Whisk together the remaining ingredients, including salt and pepper to taste. Pour the dressing onto the chicken mixture and toss well. Add more salt and pepper if needed.

**Note:** Tasted alone, the dressing may seem bitter; tossed with the chicken, it smooths out and blends perfectly.

# Intoxicating Summer Coolers

Oh, go ahead and indulge (within moderation, of course). Kick back, cool off, chill out—summer demands it. You have a lot of jazzy summer cooler choices: margarita, piña colada, sangria, wine spritzer, mint julep, mai tai, frozen daiquiri, and caipirinha, to name a few. One of the hottest (or coolest) choices is the mojito. Make one for your lovebug and one for yourself, and you might find yourselves doing the Macarena for the rest of the evening.

For each mojito you'll need 10 or 12 mint leaves, 2 teaspoons superfine sugar, 1/2 a lime, club soda, 2 ounces light rum, plus a sprig of mint and wedge of lime for garnish.

Put the mint leaves in a tall glass, add the sugar, and squeeze the lime over both. Add just a splash of club soda and muddle gently until the sugar is dissolved and the mint is crushed enough so you can smell it. Add the rum, fill the glass with ice, and stir well. Top off with more club soda and garnish with the mint sprig and lime wedge.

# Mouthwatering Colors of Summer

Watermelon Pink    Blueberry Blue

Cantaloupe Coral    Ripe Apricot

Juicy Peach    Lettuce-Leaf Green

Plum Violet    Corn Yellow

Hot Tomato    Cherry Red

# Your Dreamy Bedroom

It's summer, a heavenly time for a change of style in the bedroom—from the heavy fabrics and darker colors of winter to the light textures and romantic colors of summer. Promise it will lift your spirits, and there's no telling *what* it will do for your lovelife!

- ❀ Make up the bed with flower-patterned or striped sheets and crisp white pillowcases edged with crochet or eyelet. Stash your winter bedspread; replace with something light or white.

- ❀ Take down winter curtains and drape long lengths of pale sheer fabric over the curtain rod.

- ❀ Change the pillow shams, lampshades, throw rug. Use airy colors: ivory, white, pale pink, almond green, sky blue. Use bright flower colors: zinnia red, sunflower yellow, delphinium blue, snapdragon pink. Use cool watery colors: aquamarine, bottle green, pale turquoise.

- ❀ Take old pictures off the wall and hang botanical prints, a still life with flowers or fruit, watercolor seascapes, an embroidered sampler.

- ❀ Accessorize with clusters of candles, a tray of seashells, a bowl of potpourri.

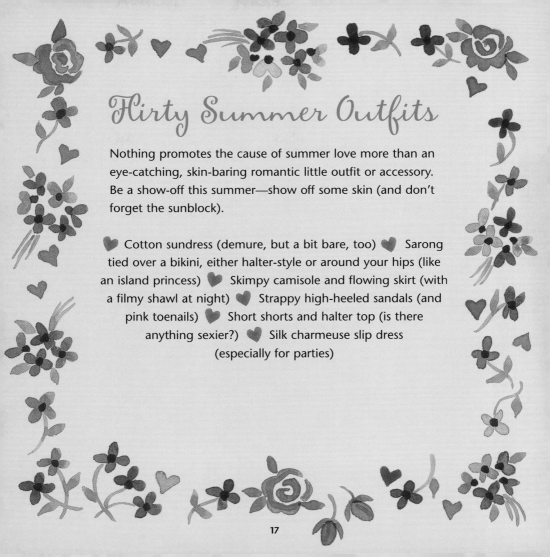

# Flirty Summer Outfits

Nothing promotes the cause of summer love more than an eye-catching, skin-baring romantic little outfit or accessory. Be a show-off this summer—show off some skin (and don't forget the sunblock).

Cotton sundress (demure, but a bit bare, too) Sarong tied over a bikini, either halter-style or around your hips (like an island princess) Skimpy camisole and flowing skirt (with a filmy shawl at night) Strappy high-heeled sandals (and pink toenails) Short shorts and halter top (is there anything sexier?) Silk charmeuse slip dress (especially for parties)

# Romantic Lighting Under the Stars

Hot, sultry days melt into velvet nights, and the most you feel like doing is relaxing on the porch or patio with a cool drink in your hand and your sweetheart by your side. A little bit of light is all you need. Try these.

❀ Decorative lanterns ❀ Hurricane lamps (preferably without the hurricane) ❀ Pillar candles set on large scallop shells (sand is nice, too) ❀ Luminarias ❀ Candles floating on water in a bowl or even in the swimming pool (add gardenias for true romance and the delicious fragrance—and wear one in your hair, while you're at it) ❀ Twinkle lights strung all over the garden ❀ Sparklers (short-lived, but pretty) ❀ And, of course, FIREFLIES and FALLING STARS!

# Summer Holidays

If you're lucky enough to be taking your vacation together in the summer, you're probably heading for a couple of weeks at the shore or in the mountains or even in Europe. Maybe you're planning a second honeymoon this year. Nice, very nice. But remember that romantic summer getaways can be simpler than that. Long or short weekends are yours for the taking—take time to be together like a couple of kids having a summer fling.

❀ Toss your bathing suits into the backseat of the car and race to a lakeside cottage. ❀ Treat yourselves to a couple of nights at a sleek motel, a romantic inn, or a cozy bed-and-breakfast. ❀ Go camping and make love in a tent or under the stars. ❀ Borrow a secluded summerhouse for a couple of days. ❀ Hop on a train, bus, or plane for a just-the-two-of-you jaunt to the big city. ❀ Check into a spa and relax together. ❀ Keep it easy and breezy—pick up and go!

# Love Tokens

Color-copy this love token or make your own, filling in the blanks with whatever delight you think your darling might enjoy. Suggestions below, but you'll surely come up with your own private ones, too.

- *A*s many hugs and kisses as you can bear
- *O*ne romantic movie and all the popcorn you can eat
- *M*y very, very special massage
- *B*reakfast in bed (with me, of course)
- *A*n afternoon of any activity your heart desires
- *A* candlelit dinner, complete with bubbly
- *A* night of painting the town red
- *A* trip to the moon on gossamer wings

Good for

# AUTUMN *Love*

Autumn is bountiful—the abundant season of the year. And in autumn, love is just as plentiful as apples! Fall is a time of fulfillment and richness, harvest and fruition, a time of golden warmth with a hint of coolness that just begs you to get out and have a wonderful time with your own adorable pumpkin. You've got orchards to visit, leaf-peeping to do, woods to scuffle through, bonfires to kindle, memories to store for the cold months ahead.

Make your autumn an autumn of love. Meet someone new under the harvest moon. Marry under a grape arbor or in a grove of oaks and maples. Have a delicious breakfast in bed with your honeybunch, with the tangy scent of leaves and wood smoke wafting in through the open window. Take your sweetheart biking, then go home and unwind in a luxurious bath. Do fall things like pumpkin carving and wine tasting and apple picking. Spend hours reminiscing during this gathering-in time of year. Give thanks for the love *in* your life and share it with the love *of* your life.

# Contents

# Fall Is for Falling in Love

Summer fades and fall begins. It's hard to let go of those days at the beach and weekends at the cottage, but there's plenty of compensation: Along with the golden light and bright days of autumn, there's a wonderful feeling of change in the air. Friends come back from wherever they've been, school starts, and suddenly your social life picks up in a new way. You meet new people—you meet one very special new person. There's the snap and crackle of romance in the crisp breeze, and you quicken to it. The two of you walk arm in arm in the autumn woods, scuffling through the dry colorful leaves, with the pungent smell of wood smoke drifting toward you. Fall is for apple cider and doughnuts, harvest and Halloween, cool evenings and comforters and cozy fires—and especially for falling in love.

It's back-to-school for you—to take a little brush-up course on your his-and-her love skills. Is there homework? You bet, from A to Z.

A     Adore your lover. Ask her to marry you.

B     Believe in him utterly. Beguile her with love.

C     Comfort him when he's unhappy. Compliment her on her accomplishments.

D     Devote time to him. Dance cheek to cheek with her.

E     Enjoy his many talents. Embrace her whenever you meet.

F     Flirt outrageously with him. Forsake all others for her.

G     Gaze at him with wonder. Give her what she most desires.

H     Handle him with care. Hold her in your arms.

I     Idealize him a little. Inspire her with your life plans.

J     Join your life to his. Joke around to make her laugh.

*K*    Know him inside out. Kneel at her feet.

*L*    Lust after him. Look into her eyes.

*M*    Marvel at his brilliance. Make love to her in the morning.

*N*    Nestle against him. Name the ten things you love most about her.

*O*    Offer him the moon. Open your heart to her.

*P*    Play sexy games with him. Prepare a delicious meal for her.

*Q*    Quicken your step when you go to meet him. Quiet her with kisses when she's upset.

*R*    Rekindle your love affair with him. Romance her with flowers.

*S*    Slip your arms around him. Savor every moment with her.

*T*    Tell him your secrets. Take her to heaven.

*U*    Unleash his passion. Understand her heart.

*V*    Validate him at all times. Venture into uncharted territory with her.

*W*    Wear something pretty for him. Wait eagerly to see her.

*X*    X-X-X your love letters to him. X-mark the spot where you first met her.

*Y*    Yearn for him. Yield your soul to her.

*Z*    Zero in on how much you love him. Zoom over and give her a great big hug.

# Autumn Bouquet

There's a whimsy to spring and summer
that scampers off when fall arrives.
Fall is earthy, grounded, solid.
The colors of autumn
are jewel-like, strong
and deep, saturated
less with light than
with energy. Autumn
foliage, shrubs, flowers are
nothing like those frothy spring
and summer blossoms of pale blue, lavender,
a hundred shades of pink. Where spring and
summer are flighty, with joy and frivolity to spare,
autumn is about harvesting, consolidating,
fortifying—gathering resources for the winter to come. Autumn is real. Autumn
is earnest. Those dark reds and purples, those rich oranges and yellows, the
variety of browns and siennas, the palette of intense greens so different from the
sprightly greens of spring and summer. Spring is a promise-maker, summer is a
spendthrift, autumn is a planner.

Love is the same: tentative and budding in its spring beginning, lavish and
carefree in its summer heat. And then comes the autumn of love—firm, reliable,
and forward-looking. Something—or someone—to count on for the future.

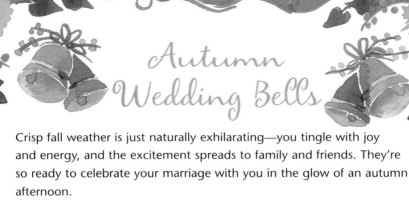

# Autumn Wedding Bells

Crisp fall weather is just naturally exhilarating—you tingle with joy and energy, and the excitement spreads to family and friends. They're so ready to celebrate your marriage with you in the glow of an autumn afternoon.

🍁 Marry in a grove of oaks and maples at the peak of leaf color, and dress your attendants in satin or taffeta in leafy colors. 🍁 Marry under a grape arbor and carry a bouquet of burgundy dahlias and wine-gold oak leaves. 🍁 Marry in a cottage garden under an ivy-twined trellis, with sunlight dappling the paths you've lined with pots of russet chrysanthemums. 🍁 Create centerpieces of champagne grapes, shiny red apples, and bright orange pumpkins. 🍁 Set each place with a tiny vase filled with strawflowers, sprigs of bittersweet, and deep green leaves. 🍁 Decorate your cake with real and chocolate leaves. 🍁 Glow with happiness under a harvest moon. 🍁 Indulge yourselves on this extraordinary day.

# Love in the Bath

Hello, hello—there's a chill in the air! Not that you need a weather excuse for luxuriating in the pagan pleasure of a hot bath with all the trimmings.

First things first: Invite your sweetheart to join you. Then carve out an hour of uninterruptible time for yourselves. Gather together your water goodies: bubble bath, fragrant bath oil, scented soap, natural sponge, back scrubber, rubber ducky. Gather together your during-the-bath goodies: candles, incense, glasses of wine, music. Gather together your after-bath goodies, too: fluffy towels, talcum powder, body cream, moisturizer. Then take the plunge. Slide into the steaming water and relax, relax, relax. Or not.

# Autumn Dinner for Two

Welcome to Saturday night and a delicious dinner for just the two of you. If you're lucky enough to have a fireplace, get that fire going and set up a little table in front of the flames. No fire? Set up your table in front of a window so you can watch the deep blue late-day sky become the star-spangled, moonlit night sky. No window? Arrange a dozen candles on the dining table and turn out the room lights. Romance is in the air.

## menu

Spinach salad with sliced mushrooms

Pork roast

Braised Red Cabbage and Apples (page 31)

Small red potatoes roasted in their skins

Pumpkin cheesecake

Wine, coffee, or tea

# Braised Red Cabbage and Apples

**3 slices lean bacon**

**1 tablespoon butter**

**3 cups shredded red cabbage**

**1 medium-large Granny Smith apple, peeled, cored, and diced**

**3 tablespoons red currant or apple jelly**

**1 tablespoon sugar**

**1 1/2 tablespoons red wine vinegar**

**Salt, fresh pepper**

In a medium skillet, cook the bacon until crisp; drain on paper towels, crumble, and set aside. Pour off most of the bacon fat and add the butter to the skillet.

Stir in the cabbage and apple and sauté over low heat until the cabbage is wilted. Stir in the remaining ingredients, including the reserved bacon, seasoning well with the salt and pepper. Cover the skillet and cook over low heat for 15 minutes, until the cabbage and apples are quite soft.

Uncover the skillet, raise the heat to medium, and cook until the liquid evaporates and the cabbage and apples are glazed. Serve hot.

# Dress-up for Grown-ups

When you're a child, October means Halloween. Now that you're a grown-up, forget all that trick-or-treat candy—what about those terrific costumes? There's no law that says only kids get to have the fun of dressing up! In public or in private, suiting up in something special can be downright exciting for lovers.

🍂 Have a costume party and invite everyone you know (no one allowed in without a disguise). 🍂 Put a sexy costume spin on your relationship (have you ever wanted to play Naughty Nurse or Daring Doctor? Cheerleader? Firefighter? Police officer?). 🍂 Wear something outrageous (a crazy hat? five-inch heels? pearls and nothing else?). 🍂 Wear something very, very skimpy (ah, the lingerie moment . . .). 🍂 Rent the right outfits and dress up like your favorite movie characters (Scarlett and Rhett? Spiderman and Catwoman?). 🍂 Cobble together the right outfits and dress up like your favorite music stars (Elvis and Cher? Dolly Parton and Bruce Springsteen?). 🍂 Go out on the town in a fabulous gown and a sensational tuxedo (knock 'em dead!).

# My Little Pumpkin

Feeling romantic this fall? Brimming over with a harvest of love for your sweet little pumpkin? Show your devotion! Buy a nice-sized hollow plastic pumpkin, the kind you see at Halloween, and stuff it full of goodies. Here are some possible love-crazy pumpkin-stuffers:

- Chocolates kisses and hugs
- Butterscotch and caramels
- Marzipan fruits or animals
- Chocolate pretzels
- Small silly toys
- Love notes
- Homemade cookies
- Brownies
- Sexy panties
- Edible body paint
- Romantic CDs
- A diamond ring

# Harvest of Love

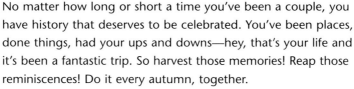

No matter how long or short a time you've been a couple, you have history that deserves to be celebrated. You've been places, done things, had your ups and downs—hey, that's your life and it's been a fantastic trip. So harvest those memories! Reap those reminiscences! Do it every autumn, together.

💜 Get a new photo album and put your latest pix into it, with dates and captions.

💜 Throw a huge party and invite everyone who's part of your history, in-state and out-of-state.

💜 Take your parents out for dinner—they're part of your history, too.

💜 Invite the members of your wedding over for a night of wedding videos—go on, fess up to all the wild and crazy behind-the-scenes stories.

💜 Make a slide show about your life together.

💜 Have a quiet, romantic dinner à deux and talk over the absolutely best moments of your relationship.

# Giving Thanks

September and October have been full and rich. But as November days grow shorter and the year moves inexorably toward its close, the landscape seems suddenly bleak, and the waning of light and warmth can change your mood to dark and cold. It can be difficult to remember exactly what there is to feel thankful for. Take time, when that happens, to take notice. Do you have family? Do you have friends? Do you have shelter, work, someone dear to come home to? Do you have someone to depend on and someone who depends on you?

On the fourth Thursday of November, look inward, but look outward, too. Remember that you're not the only one feeling chilled as winter approaches. Extra hugs, extra kisses—distribute them generously to those you cherish. Be thankful you have love to give, and be thankful for the love you get in return.

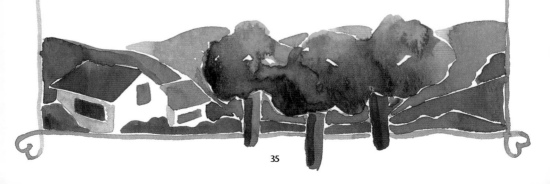

# Breakfast in Bed

You open your eyes early. Someone (guess who) has left the window open a few inches and there's an autumn chill in the bedroom. Delicious. Fresh. Invigorating. You slide out of bed quietly (don't wake up you-know-who), wrap yourself in a warm robe, and tiptoe to the kitchen. Breakfast in bed—great idea. It doesn't have to be fancy, that's not the point. What you want is some nice food coupled with a little downtime, a little snuggling, a little intimate chat—wherever it might lead. Put the coffee on, pop some good bread into the toaster. Maybe scramble up some eggs with grated cheddar cheese. Mmm, bacon, smells wonderful. A wedge of juicy melon, glass of juice, some sliced tomatoes, sure, tomatoes, why not be daring. Butter, pot of honey, what else? Find a big tray, load it up. Sneak back up the stairs to your sleeping lover. Wake him. Make him happy.

# Autumn Jaunts

Tootling around the countryside together in September and October is one of the greatest pleasures of autumn. A getaway afternoon of fresh air and fooling around is guaranteed to rekindle your romance in short order because it reminds you how much you love hanging out with each other. You have so much fun together! Now, that's worth a pumpkin or two.

🍁 Drive the scenic route to ooh and aah at the turning leaves. 🍁 Hike up a mountain and enjoy the silence and privacy. 🍁 Pack your bicycle baskets with a picnic lunch and take off as if you were eloping. 🍁 Raid a farmstand piled high with bounty—eggplants and peppers, squash and Indian corn, potatoes, beans, apples, pears, and grapes. 🍁 Buy local pumpkins for carving. 🍁 Buy a gallon of newly pressed cider for making apple martinis and hot apple toddies when you get home. 🍁 Visit a vineyard for a little wine tasting and cheese munching. 🍁 Find an isolated meadow and make love in the autumn sunshine.

# Apple-Chile Relish from Heaven

Apples and chiles love each other, so match them up in this lightly cooked condiment that is—like a good lover—sweet and mild at first, spicy and exciting as time goes by.

**2 large Granny Smith apples (1 to 1¹/₄ pounds), peeled, quartered, and cored**

**1 medium carrot, trimmed and peeled**

**1 fresh mild green chile (poblano, Anaheim, etc.), roasted and skinned**

**2 pickled jalapeños**

**¹/₄ cup cider vinegar**

**¹/₄ cup water**

**¹/₄ cup sugar**

**¹/₄ teaspoon salt**

**1 clove garlic, minced**

**¹/₄ cup minced red onion**

Chop the apples into pea-sized bits. Grate the carrot. Stem, halve, and seed the roasted green chile and the jalapeños; mince.

In a medium saucepan, simmer the vinegar, water, sugar, salt, and garlic, stirring until the sugar is dissolved. Stir in the chopped apples and continue simmering, uncovered, for 10 minutes, until the apples are tender. Stir in the grated carrot and simmer for another minute. There should be very little liquid left in the pan. Turn off the heat.

Add the minced chile, jalapeños, and onion. Stir well and allow to cool. Season with more salt if needed. Keeps well for 3 days in the fridge, getting hotter each day.

# The Rich Colors of Autumn

How glorious the colors of autumn are! How splendid it would be to capture them, to enjoy them all winter. You *can* do it, and we're not talking maple leaves pressed between sheets of waxed paper. Instead, get yourself to the yarn store pronto for skeins of amber, yellow, pumpkin, burnt orange, terra-cotta, scarlet, burgundy, magenta, moss green, hunter green, golden brown, earth brown, wheat. Make yourself a gorgeous patchwork afghan of simple knitted or crocheted squares in a cornucopia of fall colors. Voilà—autumn for as long as you want it. And be sure to make that afghan wa-a-a-ay large enough for two to cuddle under.

# WINTER *Love*

Winter is festive—the holiday season of the year. Days are shorter, of course, but nights are longer! And longer nights are optimum for parties, gatherings, and especially for love, so give lots of attention to having a good time with your sugarplum. End the year with as much excitement and delight as you two can take: holiday celebrations and winter getaways, mistletoe kisses and cold-weather cuddling, snowball fights and hot toddies to thaw you out.

Make your winter a winter of love. Take time for each other—an indoor picnic, a tree-trimming day, a Valentine dinner. Turn your home into a paradise for lovers. Give gifts from the heart. Escape to a cozy inn for rest, recreation, and romance. Squeeze in a few quiet, intimate moments for sharing your reflections on the past and the future. Start your own special traditions and make them last for dozens of winters to come.

# CONTENTS

# Loving Traditions

Lovers should have their own special traditions, started in the heat of romance and carried on through the years. The winter holidays offer dozens of deliciously romantic possibilities. Here are two.

**Christmas Tree Day:** Decide on a day for getting your tree and pick it out together *without getting into an argument*. Decorate it with ornaments that speak of love—hearts, love notes, anything you've acquired together over the years, new ornaments you buy or make together. When your tree is perfect right down to the last strand of tinsel, turn out the room lights and turn on the tree lights. Snuggle into the couch and rhapsodize over your beautiful creation.

**One Special Night:** His family, your family, your friends—they all want you for holiday occasions. But you want *each other*, too. Set aside one special night to be together, whether it's Christmas Eve, Christmas Night, or the Night After the Night After Christmas. Turn *on* the answering machine, turn *off* the TV, and be together. (And you might want to save one present for that One Special Night, too.)

# Turning Up the Heat on Romance

Baby, it's cold out there. Wouldn't you rather stay inside where you can make yourselves nice and warm?

- 💜 Have a pillow fight.
- 💜 Tickle each other until one of you yells, "Uncle!"
- 💜 Give her a massage.
- 💜 Give him a rubdown.
- 💜 Wrap up together in a big soft quilt.
- 💜 Watch a couple of romantic videos or DVDs.
- 💜 Snuggle in front of a fire.
- 💜 Sit on his lap.
- 💜 Chase her around the living room.
- 💜 Take a hot shower together.
- 💜 Neck until you've steamed up the windows, then neck some more.

# Winter Wedding Bells

A sparkling wonderland is yours when you have a winter wedding. Early sunset is an exquisite opportunity to illuminate your ceremony and reception with the romance of chandeliers, sconces, firelight, strings of fairy lights, or hundreds of candles.

Marry in the city, with a twinkling cityscape for a backdrop. Marry in the country, with a cozy fireplace in the background. Marry in a fine old college chapel, with the soaring voices of a college choir to sing you in and out. Arrive at the ceremony in a horse-drawn sleigh with jingling bells. Hold your reception in a handsome room glittering with gold, silver, and crystal. Think winter white—white roses, snowflake ornaments, white ribbons, white candles, white table linen. Garland everything in evergreens laced with red berries and red flowers. Make sure your guests feel warm and sheltered. Make merry until the sun comes up. Don't forget the mistletoe.

# The Story of Mistletoe

Actually, no one knows exactly where the kissing-beneath-the-mistletoe tradition originated. There are plenty of theories, all impossible to prove. For instance, the ancient Celts seem to have used mistletoe in marriage rites because it was thought to be an aphrodisiac, but this doesn't make much sense because ingesting mistletoe will make you pretty sick and might even kill you. Not a good idea on Marriage Night.

In the ninth century BCE, in the Babylonian-Assyrian Empire, single women apparently liked to stand beneath the decorative mistletoe at the temple of the goddess of love, waiting to be snapped up by passing bachelors. No kissing, though, because that was before kissing became popular in that part of the world.

More recently we've clung to a persistent belief that any couple who kisses under the mistletoe will get married within a year. Maybe they will, maybe they won't—or maybe we should stop worrying about the outcome and start enjoying the kisses! Maybe we should carry sprigs of mistletoe around at all times, just in case.

# Love Note in the Snow

Fill a narrow-tipped watering can with water and tint the water with food coloring. Sneak outside early in the morning and pour your heart out—with a love note written on the new snow. How about a big pink heart with both your initials inside?

# Winter Romance

Sometimes winter can feel so gloomy and disheartening. Will the days *ever* lengthen? Will the skies ever be anything but cold and gray? Will there ever be enough warmth and sunshine again in this lifetime? These are just feelings, of course, but those feelings can certainly discourage a person. And if that person happens to be your partner, it's time for you to go into loving, care-taking action.

Splurge on a few flowering houseplants— such a joy when gardens are bare and flowers really mean something. Make sure there's enough *light* in your home; bring in a few more lamps and up the wattage in the lamps you already have. Get some cheerful music going. Don't let your mate mope around; spend time with him doing some of the things he enjoys. Take her to a warm, sunny place for a few days of relief. Make love a *lot*. Do whatever it takes to help your beloved through the dark winter moments.

# Indoor Do-It-Yourself Picnic for Two

Bet you thought picnics for two were a summer-only phenomenon. You lose the bet! Move that picnic indoors—by the fire, to the living room floor, or even into bed—and recapture the delights of relaxing together over a delicious, unfussy meal. No ants, no mosquitoes, no lumpy tree roots beneath you—just music, a candle or two, and a good time.

## MENU

Salsa, corn tortilla chips

Beef fajitas:
(sliced grilled or broiled skirt steak, grilled or sautéed onions and sweet peppers, sliced avocado, chopped pickled jalapeños, chopped tomatoes, shredded lettuce)

Flour tortillas

Refried beans

Beer

# My True Love Gave to Me

Everybody (especially your favorite lady) loves gifts. Give lots!

- 💜 Twelve red roses
- 💜 Eleven chocolate kisses
- 💜 Ten CDs of romantic music
- 💜 Nine love letters
- 💜 Eight new lipsticks
- 💜 Seven days at a cozy inn
- 💜 Six romance novels
- 💜 Five fancy bath products
- 💜 Four lacy nightgowns
- 💜 Three books of love poetry
- 💜 Two ruby earrings
- 💜 And your heart, for eternity

## 52

### Weeks of Love

A new year is coming—opportunity knocks! Fifty-two bright, shiny new weeks of love! New Year's Day might just be the day you begin your preparations.

Get two square pads of Post-it notes in two different colors. Count off twenty-six of each color, one stack for you and one for him. On the back of each Post-it write down an activity you'd like to do with your partner, an idea for a date, or something sexy you'd like to try. Fold each in half, sealing it closed along the sticky edge. Every Saturday (or whatever day works best for the two of you), pull out one note (alternating colors, of course) and *do whatever the note says.*

# Tropical Paradise

Before those winter blues have a chance to put a dent in your romance, make a change! Turn your bedroom into a place you and your beloved can't wait to get to every single night—and hate leaving in the morning. You need not make major alterations; instead, put the emphasis on accessorizing.

Give the walls a quick coat of lemon yellow, almond green, or pale turquoise paint. Bring in lots of green or flowering plants. Go for color: ocean blue bedspread; bright yellow, pink, purple, red, orange throw pillows; tropical print skirts on the night tables. Fill a vase with big colorful paper or fabric flowers. Add an area rug in a bright color or a flower pattern. Drape sarong fabric over the curtain rod or use it to tie back existing curtains. Frame and hang color photos of tropical scenes—palm trees, surf, sandy beaches.

Put straw mats under lamps and plants.

# Matinee

On the afternoon after a big snowfall, grab your honeybun, get out there, and build a snowman or two. Have a snowball fight, chase each other, roll around in the white stuff. When you're really cold and wet and ready to call it a day, get warm the loving way: Take a hot bath together. Curl up under a woolly afghan. Have mulled wine or hot cocoa. See what develops.

# Hot Toddies for Chilled Bodies

These toddies will warm you from the tips of your noses to the tips of your toeses, and put you in a mellow, mellow mood. Each recipe below is for one toddy, which you should make in a warmed-up mug or thick glass.

**Note:** A jigger is a 1 1/2-ounce shot glass, equal to 3 tablespoons of liquid.

**Hot Buttered Rum:** Combine 2 jiggers dark rum, a twist of lemon peel, 1 clove, and a cinnamon stick. Add boiling cider to taste. Float a small pat of butter on top.

**Hot Lemon-Lime Toddy:** Stir together juice of 1/2 lemon, juice of 1/2 lime, and 2 tablespoons superfine sugar. Add 1 jigger whiskey or rum and top off with boiling water to taste.

**Hot Applejack Toddy:** Combine 1 jigger applejack, 1 teaspoon superfine sugar, 2 cloves, and a slice of lemon. Add boiling water to taste.

**Hot Wine Cup:** Stir together 1/4 cup red wine, juice of 1/2 lemon, 2 teaspoons superfine sugar, and a twist of lemon peel. Add boiling water to taste.

# Glad Rags

Take advantage of the winter holiday season to enchant your sweetheart with your festive, pretty, sassy, elegant outfits. Feel especially free to wear textures that feel good to the touch (*his* touch), like cashmere, angora, velvet, silk, and satin.

- Red velvet dress or skirt (short is cute)
- Winter white angora or cashmere sweater (so soft and huggable)
- Black velvet slacks (elegant!)
- Anything sparkly or glittery on top (outshine the stars)
- Flowing silk hostess pants (make an entrance)
- Shimmering earrings or necklace (crystal is beautiful)
- Lacy or embroidered jacket (very nice over a little black dress)

# Winter Getaways

Of course you can escape to warm, sunny vacation spots, but you could also choose to get into the season and go with the snow.

For a quick getaway, drive to a thrilling sledding hill and whiz down over and over (ride double-decker, for romance). Book into a hotel or inn on a frozen lake, for the fun of ice skating (or ice dancing) with your darling. Head for a cabin in a snowy forest and hole up for a weekend of making love in front of the roaring fire. Do snow skiing of any kind (don't waste those after-ski moments!). Book the honeymoon suite of a jazzy hotel for a winter weekend of city fun. Explore the snowy backwoods on snowshoes. Hike the trails of a national park. Mix hot and cold at a vacation hideaway with a hot tub (or sauna) that looks out on a snowy landscape, and spend hours relaxing together.

# Sweet Temptation

Pull together a few of these goodies to make a Valentine's Day feast for your darling. Sweets for the sweet, right?

💜 Chocolate kisses and hugs 💜 Cupcakes decorated with candy hearts 💜 Heart-shaped cake frosted in her favorite flavor 💜 Cherry cheesecake 💜 Chocolate-dipped strawberries 💜 Heart-shaped butter cookies iced in red 💜 Heart-shaped linzer cookies filled with raspberry jam 💜 Strawberry-raspberry tart 💜 Pink petit fours with red piping 💜 Bag of cinnamon redhots 💜 Heart-shaped lollipops 💜 Big heart-shaped box of the fanciest assorted chocolates you can find

# Valentine's Day Surprise

Fellas, you'll knock off her socks (and maybe one or two other garments) if you successfully execute this Valentine's Day night of romance. It takes a little planning and loving energy, but your own precious chickadee is worth it, isn't she?

**Two weeks before V-Day:** Send her an e-mail or card inviting her to dinner on February 14. Inform her firmly that she will do nothing (not even bring wine), while you will do everything.

**One week before V-Day:** Call or, even better, stop in at your favorite restaurant and arrange for a lovely meal you can *pick up* on V-Day, *take home*, and *reheat safely*. Be sure you get reheating instructions you can actually follow. Don't forget to order dessert.

**Two days before V-Day:** Buy candles (pink tapers or red pillars are nice) and wine. Clean up the house (yes, you must clean up the house). Set the dining table with a *tablecloth* and *cloth napkins*, borrowed if necessary. You're on a roll now: Put out plates, flatware, water glasses, and wineglasses.

**One day before V-Day:** Buy flowers—*not roses* (everybody buys roses). Get something interesting, like a mixed bouquet in pink, red, and white. Put the flowers in a vase on the table.

**V-Day:** Pick up the food and have it ready to reheat. Spruce yourself up. Turn down the room lights and fire up the candles. Put music on. Hover near the door nervously. When she arrives, take a breath, relax, and enjoy.

# SPRING *Love*

Spring is hopeful—the promising season of the year. Every living thing begins to bloom, and love does, too. There's more time for you and your sweetpea to be together in the lengthening days and breathtakingly romantic evenings. You're so glad to be alive now that spring is really, really here. Whimsy captures you, and you ply each other with champagne cocktails, chocolates, sweet words, and slow dances in the honeysuckle-scented dark.

Make your spring a spring of love. Romance your darling with the very special flowers of spring, the fleeting daffodils and hyacinths and lilacs. Make him a spring dinner he'll remember all year. Tell her how frisky you feel and then fly her off to Paris for Easter. Marry in a garden of magnificent magnolias and dogwoods. Sprinkle your path with flower petals—tokens of love—now and always.

# CONTENTS

# The Romance of Spring Flowers

Green spikes of crocus, hyacinth, and daffodil poke hopefully out of the newly softening ground beside the forsythia's yellow-flower-laden branches. Magnolias explode into bloom and the ivory and pink dogwoods aren't far behind. Before you can think twice, lilac bushes will be a froth of exquisitely scented blooms, and the pale gray wisteria vines will cascade with lavender. Bring your love a bouquet of spring flowers to gladden her heart.

# Blissful Moments

The advent of spring makes you feel as if you've been sprung from cold, rainy Muddy Weather Jail. If you were a pair of lambs, you'd frolic. If you were a pair of birds, you'd swoop and warble and build a nest. But it's great enough simply being the two of you during these newly sweet, softening days and warmer nights. So spring forward and do some playing!

💜 Ride a bike-for-two. 💜 Have a game of tag. 💜 Take a ferry ride. 💜 Play spin-the-bottle and post office. 💜 Blow the fuzz off dandelions. 💜 Walk on an empty beach, hold hands, cuddle on a sand dune—just a couple of lovers and a perfect spring day to spend together.

# Love Is in the Air

Your lover rests his cheek on your hair, presses his face to your neck, inhaling deeply. "You smell wonderful," he says softly, holding you close. He whispers, "You smell like roses." Or lilies or lilacs or vanilla or cinnamon. Your perfume sends a subtle message to others, but the language of your scent speaks eloquently to him. It draws him to you. Fragrance is magic, and you've bewitched him.

# G♥ds and G♥ddesses ♥f L♥ve

Aphrodite and Eros were the Greek goddess and god of love. You may also know them by their Roman names—Venus and Cupid. Heavens, they packed a wallop.

Aphrodite was not only the goddess of love, but the goddess of beauty, fertility, and sexual rapture (and she had sidelines in marriage, family life, war, and the sea). She was irresistible to men: She wore a magic girdle that caused the poor fellows to fall hopelessly in love with her or with anyone to whom she loaned the girdle. She loved gaiety and glamour, and we have her to thank for the concept of aphrodisiacs.

Eros was a veritable decathlon athlete of love: He personified physical passion, playful love, tender love, romantic love, and just about any other kind of love you can think of. To the Greeks he was a winged young man with a youth-sized bow and arrows; to the Romans he was a chubby, naked child with miniature bow and arrows—the Cupid you've seen on a thousand Valentine's Day cards. He was mischievous: He made the victims of his magic arrows fall madly in love (often with the wrong people) and then tortured them with the agony of it all.

So look out! If you've been tapped by Aphrodite or pierced by Eros this spring, you're in for a wild ride.

# Bubbly Love Potion

In spring a young man's fancy lightly turns to thoughts of love, doesn't it? Or does it? It's supposed to, but just in case he's slow off the mark, you might want to offer him a little encouragement. Instead of brewing up seven drops of this and nine drops of that or feeding him with dates, figs, and pomegranates or rubbing him down with aphrodisiac essential oils, you *could* do it the easy way: Take out that bottle of champagne you've been saving and build him a classic champagne cocktail. That should do the trick.

For each cocktail you'll need 1 sugar cube, angostura bitters, 1 scant ounce (about 2 tablespoons) brandy or cognac, and champagne. Simply drop the sugar cube into a champagne flute and soak with bitters. Add the brandy and top off with champagne.

# Seduction by Irresistible Chocolate Squares

You've tried the bubbly love potion on page 64, you've tried the perfume, the dim lighting, the sexy little black dress. If all these wiles fail, get real: Snare him with chocolate.

**¹/₂ cup (1 stick) unsalted butter**

**¹/₂ cup light corn syrup**

**5 ounces high-quality semisweet chocolate (such as Callebaut, Lindt, Valrhona, or Ghirardelli)**

**³/₄ cup sugar**

**1 teaspoon vanilla extract**

**3 eggs**

**1 cup flour stirred with ¹/₄ teaspoon salt**

Preheat the oven to 350° F; grease and flour a 9 x 9-inch baking pan.

In a medium-size saucepan over low heat, melt the butter, corn syrup, and chocolate, stirring until blended and smooth. Transfer to a large bowl and stir in the sugar and vanilla. Beat in the eggs one at a time. Gradually add the flour, blending well after each addition. Spread the batter in the prepared pan.

Bake for 30 to 33 minutes, until the top is dry and crisp, and a toothpick inserted in the center of the pan comes out almost clean. Allow the pan to cool completely on a wire rack. Run a sharp knife around the edge, then cut into twenty-five squares (five squares by five squares), wiping the knife blade between cuts.

# Spring Wedding Movies

Wedding season is hovering on the horizon. If you're thinking about having a nervous breakdown over it—a distinct possibility whether you're the bride, the groom, the parents, or just an interested party—you need a great big dose of humor and encouragement (and maybe a good cry, too). Get your medicine right here.

*Father of the Bride* (both old and new versions)

*Runaway Bride*

*Betsy's Wedding*

*The Wedding Planner*

*My Big Fat Greek Wedding*

*My Best Friend's Wedding*

*Muriel's Wedding*

*Four Weddings and a Funeral*

*Monsoon Wedding*

*Royal Wedding*

*Much Ado About Nothing*

# Spring Wedding Bells

Something old, something new, something borrowed, something blue—for a spring wedding, of course. The *old* winter lingers just a bit, but the *new* spring is bursting forth like a happy dream. It feels as if you've *borrowed* all the joy of heaven, and the tender *blue* sky arches benevolently over your long-awaited day.

❀ Marry in a lovely inn with a garden in early bloom, a bursting-forth of dogwood, magnolia, forsythia, lilac. ❀ Marry in a grand cathedral, with organ music that lifts every heart to romantic heights.
❀ Marry under a canopy made by your dearest friends, supported at the four corners by your favorite relatives. ❀ Carry white tulips, lilies-of-the-valley, gardenias. ❀ Have your attendants wear picture hats trimmed with fresh spring flowers. ❀ Decorate the reception room with pastel-colored paper butterflies and satin ribbons. ❀ Think lavender and pale yellow (spring is the yellow-and-purple time!).
❀ Serve strawberries and champagne. ❀ Strew the aisles with petals of roses and peonies. ❀ Delight in every moment of this splendid event.

# Lovebirds

If you were a dove, you'd find your true love and mate for life. If you were a Great Horned Owl or a Canada Goose or an American Bald Eagle, you'd do the same. Swans are in the club, too, and so are a lot of penguins and ovenbirds. Bird loyalty and bird faithfulness are high values among these flocks, whatever the biological reason might be.

Contrary to popular myth, lovebirds (a species of parrot) are not necessarily maters-for-life. But if you buy and keep a pair of lovebirds, they'll bond closely and probably pay very little attention to anyone else. Sound like any other couples you know?

# Dancing in the Dark

On a warm spring night, take your CDs out to the patio, backyard, park, or secluded clearing in the woods, and dance to your favorite slow songs. Tony Bennett, Frank Sinatra, Ella Fitzgerald, Norah Jones, Ray Charles, Steve Tyrell, Diana Krall, Nat King Cole, Carmen McRae, Etta James, Rod Stewart, Sam Cooke—whoever sings to you of love. The deep silken dark, the fragrant caressing air, the music that echoes the rhythm of your heart. Romantic beyond romantic.

# Spring Dinner for Two

Celebrate the arrival of spring with this lovely lovers' dinner of traditionally springlike treats. Once upon a time these foods—lamb, asparagus, strawberries—were seasonal specialties, but no longer. Oh, well, maybe it's not the worst thing in the world if food, like love, is year-round.

Serve the smoked salmon appetizer in the living room before dinner, accompanied by your cocktail or wine of choice. Move to the candlelit dining room for the rest of the meal.

## MENU

Baby radishes

Smoked salmon on buttered black bread
with honey-mustard or dill sauce

Baby lamb chops

Asparagus with butter

Risotto with minced parsley

Strawberries on meringue shells, topped
with whipped cream

# Romance at Dawn

You didn't know you were going to be awake so early, but now that you are, there's a miracle waiting to happen—sunrise! Wake your partner with kisses, get up, go outside together. Sunrise is especially delicious in spring, when it's still cool (even chilly) in the morning, when dew can be like ice water on your bare feet, the grass is tender and soft, the birds are wild with delight.

It's so quiet, even in a city. The sky is changing from moment to moment, a romantic palette of spring colors—pale blue, pale turquoise, pink, yellow, lavender, like spring flowers. Brushstrokes of white accent the satiny fabric of sky. You can hear hints of sound—a low hum of traffic, a lapping of water, a sh-sh-sh of leaves in the breeze. Stand still and be in the moment. Then go home and make love.

# Spring Break

College kids aren't the only ones who need spring break. You and your partner need a little R-and-R, too, don't you? A March weekend of peace and quiet together. An April week far away from family, friends, jobs, responsibilities. Ten May days of good food, fun activities, and plenty of romance. Bulletin: Spring is a great time to bolt because it's off season at most beaches, the Caribbean, even Europe.

❀ Take a cruise and do *everything* the package has to offer (and a few things the social director might not have planned). ❀ See the azaleas and rhododenrons at a famous garden spot. ❀ Rent a cabin in the woods and set the place on fire with your passion. ❀ Hole up in a four-star hotel for a weekend of room service and pampering. ❀ Go to the shore and be *alone*. ❀ Fly your love affair to Barcelona, Rome, or Prague. ❀ Pack your bags, grab your sweetie, and leave home!

# Come-Hither Jewelry

It's spring! Time to shed those winter doldrums and those layers of layers and strut your stuff. Time to doll up and send your guy a couple of come-hither, let's-make-love glances. Pay no attention to the fashionistas—sexy is how you and your partner define it, even where jewelry is concerned. Wear whatever makes you tingle.

❀ Delicate ankle bracelet (on your delicate ankle)
❀ Pearl necklace (and nothing else) ❀ Crystal bracelet
(for sparkle) ❀ Gold chain around your bare waist (under your
clothes) ❀ Big silver hoop earrings (like a wild gypsy)
❀ Armful of bangles (more of the gypsy in you) ❀ Jewel studs
for your ears (restrained elegance) ❀ ID necklace or bracelet
(that he gave you) ❀ Phi Beta Kappa pin (smart is sexy)
❀ Macaroni necklace (made by your beloved child)
❀ Diamond ring (on your finger)
❀ Gold wedding band (ditto)

# The Romantic Gesture

There's no reason for it. No special occasion, no social requirement, no obligation. The romantic gesture is an act of love, pure and simple—unexpected, very, very personal, and straight from the heart. It whispers, "I love you and I'm thinking of you."

- Bring her a huge spring bouquet of lilacs, tulips, or daffodils—or all three!

- Send her a small gift with a card that says "Just because I love you."

- Telephone your love in the middle of a difficult workday, to encourage him.

- Leave a love letter for your angel—under his pillow, taped to his steering wheel, in his briefcase.

- E-mail her a sentimental message—ten times in one day.

- Give him a bottle of champagne to celebrate his very existence.

- Write a poem that praises her to the April skies.

- Bring home his absolutely favorite food—splurge a little!

- Think hard about what romantic gesture would make your lover smile with pleasure this spring—and do it.